Follow That Truck!
A Story Book

by Jim Razzi • illustrated by Paul Richer

Copyright © 1987 Fisher-Price, division of The Quaker Oats Company. All rights reserved.
Fisher-Price, Little People and Awning Design are trademarks of The Quaker Oats Company
and are used under license. Program created by Parachute Press, Inc. Published by
Marvel Books, 387 Park Avenue South, New York, N.Y. 10016
Printed in the U.S.A.
ISBN 0-87135-201-X

Here is a truck carrying trees.
Let's follow that tree truck
and see where it goes.

It goes to the wood factory.
Buzzzzzzzz! The tree is cut
into nice even pieces.

Put the pieces on another truck.
Let's follow that wood truck.

It goes to the furniture factory.
Bang, bang! The pieces are
made into furniture.

Put the furniture on another truck.
Let's follow that furniture truck!

7

It goes to the furniture store.
You buy the furniture.

Put the furniture on another truck.
Let's follow that store truck!

It goes to your house!
How do you like your new chair?

Here is a truck carrying cows.
Let's follow that cow truck!

It goes to a dairy farm.
The cows get off.
They are going to live with Farmer Brown.
Moooo! Farmer Brown milks the cows.

Put the milk into another truck.
Let's follow that milk truck.

It goes to the dairy.
Swoosh! Some of the milk is
poured into containers.
Churn! A part of the milk is
churned into butter.
Whrrrrrr! A part of the milk is
made into ice cream.

14

Put the ice cream on an ice-cream truck.
Let's follow that ice-cream truck!

15

It goes to your block!
Yummy! What is your favorite flavor?

16

Here is a truck carrying metal.
Let's follow that metal truck!

It goes to the metal factory.
The factory is called a rolling mill.
Crunch! Heavy rollers roll the metal
into sheets.

Put the sheets of metal on a truck.
Let's follow that sheet metal truck!

It goes to the automobile factory.
Clang, bang! The sheets are used
to make cars and trucks.

Put the cars on a car truck.
Let's follow that car truck!

It goes to the car lot.
You sit in the car.
Would you like to take a ride?

Here is a truck carrying wool.
Let's follow that wool truck!
Where does it go?

23

It goes to the cloth mill.
Spin, whizzzz!
The wool is made into cloth.

24

Put the cloth on a truck.
Let's follow that cloth truck!

It goes to the clothing factory.
Snip, snap!
The cloth is made into clothing.

Put the clothing on a truck.
Let's follow that clothing truck!

It goes to the clothing store.
Now you have a new dress or pants for school!

Here is a truck carrying paper.
Let's follow that paper truck!

It goes to the printer.
Clickety, clack! The printer makes
books with the paper.

Put the books on a truck.
Let's follow that book truck!

It goes to a book store.
Now you can choose books
to look at and read.